A Brief Guide to Critical Thinking: The Foundations of Ethico-Philosophical Reasoning, Second Edition

Terry Sader, Ph.D.

Butler Community College

Terry Sader, Ph.D.
A Brief Guide to Critical Thinking: The Foundations of Ethico-Philosophical Reasoning,
Second Edition

Executive Editors:
Michele Baird, Maureen Staudt &
Michael Stranz

Project Development Manager:
Linda deStefano

Sr. Marketing Coordinators:
Lindsay Annett and Sara Mercurio

Production/Manufacturing Manager:
Donna M. Brown

Production Editorial Manager:
Dan Plofchan

Pre-Media Services Supervisor:
Becki Walker

Rights and Permissions Specialist:
Kalina Ingham Hintz

Cover Image
Getty Images*

The Adaptable Courseware Program
consists of products and additions to
existing Thomson products that are
produced from camera-ready copy.
Peer review, class testing, and
accuracy are primarily the responsibility
of the author(s).

ISBN-13: 978-1-4266-3631-8
ISBN-10: 1-4266-3631-8

International Divisions List

Asia (Including India):
Thomson Learning
(a division of Thomson Asia Pte Ltd)
5 Shenton Way #01-01
UIC Building
Singapore 068808
Tel: (65) 6410-1200
Fax: (65) 6410-1208

Australia/New Zealand:
Thomson Learning Australia
102 Dodds Street
Southbank, Victoria 3006
Australia

Latin America:
Thomson Learning
Seneca 53
Colonia Polano
11560 Mexico, D.F., Mexico
Tel (525) 281-2906
Fax (525) 281-2656

Canada:
Thomson Nelson
1120 Birchmount Road
Toronto, Ontario
Canada M1K 5G4
Tel (416) 752-9100
Fax (416) 752-8102

UK/Europe/Middle East/Africa:
Thomson Learning
High Holborn House
50-51 Bedford Row
London, WC1R 4LS
United Kingdom
Tel 44 (020) 7067-2500
Fax 44 (020) 7067-2600

Spain (Includes Portugal):
Thomson Paraninfo
Calle Magallanes 25
28015 Madrid
España
Tel 34 (0)91 446-3350
Fax 34 (0)91 445-6218

Table of Contents

Life and Reason...5

Argument and Reason..7

Rules of Reason 8

Exercise 1: Arguments and Validity 10

Exercise 2: More arguments and validity...11

Argument Forms..12

Formal Fallacies 13

Exercise 3: Argument Forms and Fallacies..14

Exercise 4: More Argument Forms and Fallacies 15

Argument and Truth 16

Deduction vs. Induction..16

RET 17

Informal Fallacies 19

Exercise 5: Informal Fallacies...23

Exercise 6: More Informal Fallacies 24

On Scientific Hypothesis 25

On Analogy..26

On Guarding Terms 27

On Suppressed Premises 29

Exercise 7: Suppressed Premises...31

Exercise 1: Answer Key...32

Exercise 3: Answer Key..33

Exercise 5: Answer Key..34

Exercise 7: Answer Key..35

Acknowledgements

Many thanks go to Dr. Regina Turner for her very helpful review and advice on both form and content. This guide could also not have been completed without the patience and support of my wife Angela, and our two daughters, Caitlin and Sydney.

Life and Reason

Imagine yourself discussing an important issue with a friend (for example, to join her in becoming vegetarian). She wants you to change your mind about this issue and is giving you arguments that she is right (for example, the moral treatment of animals and better health for you). Should you change your mind? How do you know when you ought to be convinced by her claims? Are there some criteria to which you can appeal to make a reasonable judgment? Or are we simply left to our own opinions, feelings and attitudes? Before deciding, we should also remember that we do seem to recognize when someone does not, and should not, convince us. For example, if she tells you that you should become vegetarian because you are a Republican, most of us would recognize that as bad reasoning; what does your political party affiliation have to do with your eating habits? This suggests that we intuitively recognize a right way and a wrong way of thinking things through and making judgments. But our rough intuitions of what is good reasoning can also mislead us. That is, if you don't have a clear understanding of sound reasoning and how it works, it is possible to mistake a judgment based on emotional reaction for sound reasoning. Furthermore, even if your judgment is sound, if you are unable to articulate the reasonable basis for that judgment, it may be perceived as merely an emotional reaction and thus lacking rational justification. Good critical thinking requires an understanding of how basic reason works.

Thus there is good reason for taking some time at the beginning of our study of philosophy and ethics to familiarize ourselves with the basic understanding and skills required to reflect effectively on the various positions and justifications presented in this course. I suggest we start by reflecting on two fundamental aspects of critical thinking:

1. *The Universality of the Standards of Reason:* rational reflection entails an appeal to rules or standards that everyone should acknowledge--what I refer to as the "standards of reason." These standards are not some mere contrivance of philosophers; rather, they are the laws of thought and reason that have been discovered by philosophers and logicians (indeed, Plato and Aristotle may have been the first to suggest that there are right and wrong ways of arriving at a conclusion). These standards simply are the way we humans think, when we are thinking correctly. Indeed, it is not difficult to observe when someone is not thinking properly. For example, if I attribute the loss of my job to the planets being out of alignment, most people would suggest that an irrational explanation because the location of the planets seems irrelevant to most jobs. Thus, relevancy seems a rational standard that we all expect from one another, i.e., a universal standard. Logicians are tasked with discovering and codifying these standards and their work continues today. Philosophy, in particular, is bound by and makes the greatest use of these standards, as we will see.

The first standard we will study is especially powerful: validity. We will see that this concept captures our notions of relevance and the rational connections between various positions. The power of validity resides in the way it defines how we can start with a set of propositions and then derive a judgment that anyone can recognize as the only possible judgment that could be drawn from those claims. That is, this concept describes how our beliefs can be related in such a way as to demand a particular position. Thus the concept of validity is a powerful one for reconciling opposing views or, at least, for providing understanding of the rational basis for differences. As we will see, however, its application is often difficult. This concept will be discussed in detail in the following lectures and chapters. The important thing to note here is that this is a standard that can and should be expected of any rational being, even if they do not always meet it--i.e., it is universal.

The second standard we will study is the expectation of truth. That is, we all recognize that falsehoods should not convince us of someone's position. Thus we should also have some understanding of how those expectations can be met, as well as the many ways that our expectations for truth can be disappointed.

2. *The Utility of the Standards of Reason:* beyond the universal aspects of these logical rules (or perhaps because of them), critical thinking skills provide a very practical tool for resolving conflicts, analyzing problems, discovering the truth, etc. All of these pursuits demand a reliable and stable process; irrational conflict resolutions tend to merely postpone the problem, and analysis and truth are both rational concepts--thus their very nature implies an appeal to the standards of reason. Our understanding of logic has come a long way since Aristotle, the father of logic, and lends a good deal of certitude to our explanations when used properly. Consider for yourself, would you rather be given a rational justification for a claim or would you rather be told that that is just the way it is (e.g., "because I said so!" or "sit down and shut up" or "agree with me or die")? Indeed, without the tools of reason to help us decide and convince others, violence, emotion and isolation seem our only other options to resolve conflict. Thus the study of logic presents us with a practical skill for determining the rational choice, decision, or belief; everyday decisions and beliefs may not result from a logical analysis, but they can often be attributed to that process having taken place at some time. Furthermore, since these standards of reason are universal, they provide us with the best means for convincing others of the proper decision or belief and allow them to convince us.

Argument and Reason

Logic is the study of reason and the rational rules of judgment. Logic studies and helps define the rules by which we reason. For the purposes of this philosophy course, we will look at only a couple of rules and formulas to help us understand the upcoming philosophical arguments. However, the student may wish, at some point, to take a logic course to inquire further into this formal inquiry about reason.

Reason is universal and, indeed, is a defining property of humanity. Aristotle calls us the "reasoning animal." The universality of reason is important to us because if we can isolate and appropriately use the rules by which reason works, we can have some assurance that other reasonable persons will agree with our conclusions and that we will understand their conclusions. That is, if we are both behaving rationally, and I follow the rules of reason to convince you of a claim, then you should be convinced. There is no "different" way of reasoning for different people. If there were, we would have no hope of ever understanding one another.

Argument is the purest expression of reason and therefore is the best vehicle by which to study reason. While other forms of expression certainly engage in the various aspects and requirements of reason, argument engages in nothing else but the practical exercise of reason. Indeed, the argument is the way in which philosophers convey their ideas. Any idea worth listening to should be accompanied by reasons for believing it to be true, i.e., an argument or justification. Thus:

> 1. An argument consists of a position (thesis or conclusion) supported by reasons (premises).

> 2. We should look for and use *warranting connectives* to guide us. Warranting connectives are words (sign posts) to help us determine what the premises are and what the conclusion is. (Thus, there are two kinds of warranting connectives: reason or premise indicators and conclusion indicators.) You should look for these when analyzing an argument and use them when constructing your own argument. Remember, the point of any argument is to convince; therefore anything we can do to make the argument clearer and more understandable is desirable.

>> a. Examples of *premise indicators*: 'because', 'since', 'for'.

>> b. Examples of *conclusion indicators*: 'therefore', 'thus', 'so', 'in conclusion'.

>> c. While the conditional statement (if…,then…) is not a true warranting connective, it does set the pattern for an argument as we'll see when we examine the argument forms modus ponens, modus tollens and hypothetical syllogism.

The Rules of Reason

Logicians call a convincing argument 'Sound' and this is the goal of any justification. **Soundness** is essential for the argument to be a good, convincing argument (i.e. a good inference). Therefore:

1. Definition: Soundness is a *valid* argument with *true premises*.

2. Soundness is the standard for all arguments, not just philosophical ones.

3. This definition of soundness establishes the two basic standards (Rules of Reason) for evaluation of arguments: *validity* and *truth of the premises*. We will first discuss the concept of validity.

Validity refers to the deductive part of the argument. That is, validity refers to the expectation that when our statements are related in the right way they lead to one and only one reasonable conclusion.

1. Definition: **An argument is valid if and only if it is *not possible* for the premises to be true and the conclusion false.**

2. This definition is about the *form* of the argument, i.e. how the argument is stated.

3. Either an argument is valid or invalid; there is no in-between. *If an argument is invalid it should be rejected immediately.*

4. The following are examples of valid and invalid arguments (consider for yourself, which of these meets the above definition of validity):

a. All men are mortal. Therefore, Socrates is mortal.

b. Socrates is a man. Therefore, Socrates is mortal.

c. All men are mortal. Socrates is a man. Therefore, Socrates is mortal.

d. All men are mortal. Socrates is mortal. Therefore, Socrates is a man.

e. Socrates is a man. Socrates is mortal. Therefore, all men are mortal.

f. If Socrates is a man, then Socrates is mortal. Socrates is a man. Therefore, Socrates is mortal.

The question to ask about each of the preceding arguments is **"Can we imagine, in any way, that the premises are true and still believe that the conclusion could be false?"** If we apply that question to our examples we should find that argument 'a' is not valid because even if all men are mortal, that Socrates is mortal could be false since we haven't said what Socrates is.

Argument 'b' is also invalid because even though it says that Socrates is a man, it does not say that men are mortal.

Argument 'c' is valid because there is simply no way to imagine that Socrates is mortal could be false, given the truth of the first two statements (premises).

However, argument 'd' is invalid because Socrates might be my cat--nothing has been said to rule this out.

Argument 'e' is invalid because the mortality of one man should not be enough to convince us that all men are mortal.

There should be no way that you can imagine that the premises of argument 'f' are true and not believe the conclusion, i.e., 'f' is valid.

Work Exercise 1 on page 10 for determining arguments and validity and then review your answers with Exercise 1 Answer Key—see page 32.

Exercise 2 will be assigned by your instructor.

Exercise 1: Arguments and validity.

Determine: 1) Which of the following is an argument and 2) Which of the arguments is valid according to the definition of validity.

a) Most cats are smart. Garfield is a cat. So, Garfield must be smart.

b) Either I will go to the party tonight or I will study at the library. Since I'm not going to the party, I will be studying at the library.

c) You can fool some of the people all of the time, and all of the people some of the time. But you can't fool all of the people all of the time.

d) All dogs are dumb. Snoopy is a dog. So, Snoopy must be dumb.

e) If the election were held today, Kerry would win. But the election is not being held today. So, Kerry will not win.

f) If the election were held today, Bush would win. But Bush is not winning. So, the election must not be held today.

Exercise 2: More arguments and validity.

Determine: 1) Which of the following is an argument and 2) Which of the arguments is valid according to the definition of validity.

1. Some people believe in global warming; some do not. But there is growing evidence that global warming is occurring.

2. I will either study for my philosophy test or go to the concert. I will not go to the concert, so I will study for my philosophy test.

3. Most people like baseball. Julian is a person, so he must like baseball.

4. All college students drive cars. Everyone who drives a car has a driver's license. So every college student must have a driver's license.

5. When someone plays with fire, they get burned. Johnny is playing with fire, hence he is going to get burned.

6. Since nobody likes to lose and Sally is losing, Sally does not like what is happening.

7. If there is evidence for life on Mars, then we should detect moisture. But we haven't detected moisture on Mars, so there cannot be evidence for life on Mars.

8. If Intelligent Design theory is correct, there should be evidence of supernatural causes. However, there is no evidence of supernatural causes, therefore Intelligent Design theory is not correct.

9. All prayers are answered. Mary prayed last night, so her prayer will be answered.

10. When it rains, the street floods. The street is flooding so it must be raining.

Argument Forms

Standard argument forms have been identified to reduce our reliance on the above definition of validity. That is, if an argument has one of the following forms, we know that it is always valid. You should look for these forms when reading arguments and use them in your own arguments; they guarantee validity, which is half the battle! This list is by no means exhaustive--there are whole books devoted to nothing more than listing the various forms of reasoning. However, these are the most common ways of arguing and should be helpful for this course.

Modus Ponens: If A, then B. A. So, B.

Example: If it rains, then I'll bring an umbrella. It is raining. So, I brought an umbrella.

Modus Tollens: If A, then B. Not B. So, Not A.

Example: If it rains, then I'll bring an umbrella. I did not bring an umbrella. So, it is not raining.

Hypothetical Syllogism: If A, then B. If B, then C. So, if A, then C. (Notice there is no limit to the number of premises for this kind of syllogism.)

Example: If it rains, I'll bring an umbrella. If I bring an umbrella, I'll have to buy an umbrella. So, if it rains, I'll have to buy an umbrella.

Disjunctive Syllogism: Either A or B. Not A. So, B.

Example: Either we'll eat pizza or get a hamburger. We won't get a pizza. So, we'll eat a hamburger.

Categorical Syllogisms

    a. Universal Syllogism: All A is B. All B is C. So, All A is C.

    Example: All Butler County students drive to class. All drivers have a driver's license. So, All Butler County students have a driver's license.

    b. Particular Syllogism: All A is B. C is A. So, C is B.

    Example: All men are mortal. Socrates is a man. So Socrates is mortal.

Formal Fallacies

Formal Fallacies have also been identified. These are common mistakes in reasoning that should be avoided. If you discover that someone is employing one of these forms of reasoning, her argument should be rejected immediately as an example of bad reasoning. Again, this list is, by no means, exhaustive. However, these are some of the more common mistakes in formal reasoning.

Affirming the Consequent: If A, then B. B. So, A.

Example: If it rains, I'll bring an umbrella. I brought an umbrella. So, it must be raining. (Ask yourself, is the conclusion necessary given the premises?)

Denying the Antecedent: If A, then B. Not A. So, Not B.

Example: If it rains, I'll bring an umbrella. It is not raining. So, I did not bring an umbrella. (Do the premises rule out other reasons for bring an umbrella?)

Disjunctive Fallacy: Either A or B. A. So, not B.

Example: You may help yourself to either the fridge or the cupboards while you house sit for me. You get a drink from the fridge. So you now cannot get anything from the cupboards? Is that what I had in mind? (What if I meant that both options were available?)

Study the differences between the Valid Argument Forms and the Formal Fallacies--be sure that you can distinguish one from the other!

Work the following Exercise 3 for Argument Forms and Formal Fallacies on page 14 and then review your answers with Exercise 3 Answer Key—see page 33.

Exercise 4 will be assigned by your instructor.

Exercise 3: Argument Forms and Formal Fallacies.

Indicate which of the standard argument forms is being used or which formal fallacy is being committed.

1. If bacteria is in the egg salad, then the guests will become ill. The guests have not become ill. Hence, bacteria is not in the egg salad.

2. Sally is either a sophomore or a junior. Sally is not a junior. Hence, Sally is a sophomore.

3. If Joe winks at Sally, then Joe is interested in dating her. Joe winks at Sally. Hence, Joe is interested in dating her.

4. The universe is the result of chance, or it is the result of design. The evidence suggests the universe is not the result of chance. Hence, it is likely that the universe is the result of design.

5. If there are virtuous leaders, then there will be virtuous citizens. There are not virtuous leaders. Hence, there are not virtuous citizens.

6. Sally is bored or is sick. She is not sick. So she must be bored.

7. If Sally studies for the test, then she will pass. She does not study for the test. Hence, she will not pass.

8. If we spend enough money, then poverty will end. Poverty has not ended. Therefore, we haven't spent enough money.

9. I will either go on a diet or have my pants altered. If I go on a diet, then I'll be too hungry to study well. I must study well. Thus, I will not go on a diet, but rather have my pants altered.

10. I'll either go to the Rocky Mountains or stay home and read. If I want to save money, then I will stay home and read. I don't want to save money. So I won't stay home and read. Hence, I'll go to the Rocky Mountains.

11. If I lie to the Grand Jury, I'll go to jail. But if I go to jail, then I won't be able to care for my family. So if I lie to the Grand Jury, then I won't be able to care for my family.

12. If I pass my Philosophy class, then I'll graduate on time. I did graduate on time. So I must have passed Philosophy.

13. Everyone here is a BCCC student. Every BCCC student drives a car. Therefore, everyone here drives a car.

Exercise 4: More Argument Forms and Formal Fallacies.

Indicate which of the standard argument forms is being used or which formal fallacy is being committed.

1. I'll either graduate in the spring or enroll for fall classes. I am enrolling in fall classes, so I must not be graduating in the spring.

2. If there is an early frost, my flowers will die. Since there was an early frost, my flowers have died.

3. If there is time, we can play some ball before heading home. We're playing ball before going home so there must be enough time.

4. When we get home, we'll have supper. We are not having supper. Thus we are not yet home.

5. If a person reads the assignment and comes to class prepared, they will be successful. Tom did not read the assignment and is not prepared for class. Therefore, Tom cannot be successful in this class.

6. If I study Philosophy, I will understand the world and my place in it better. If I better understand the world and my role, I will live a better life. So if I study Philosophy, I will live a better life.

7. Anyone who is educated appreciates philosophy. John is an educated person, so he must appreciate philosophy.

8. Either we'll go sailing or attend the museum exhibit. If we go sailing, we'll have to wake up very early to prepare the boat. We will not be getting up early. Thus we will not be going sailing, so we will attend today's museum exhibit.

9. Sally will either go to the party or eat supper at home. If Sally wants to see Jimmy, she will go to the party. So Sally will go to the party and thus not eat supper at home.

10. If I pass my Philosophy class, I can graduate on time. If I can graduate on time, I can relax this summer. So, if I pass my Philosophy class, I can relax this summer. I am passing Philosophy, hence I am going to relax this summer.

Argument and Truth

Introductory discussions of inductive and deductive logic are often misleading in their treatment of differences between these two characteristics of reason. Too often they imply that deductive and inductive arguments are two different kinds of argument. Actually, induction and deduction merely analyze two different aspects of argumentation.

Deduction vs. Induction

The clearest difference between these two aspects of argument, and the most important for our purposes, is in how deduction and induction are assessed when evaluating an argument. It is important to note that since deduction refers to the formal characteristics of an argument, i.e., validity, it is assessed absolutely as a matter of the definition of validity. Induction, on the other hand, is assessed as a matter of the degree or strength of evidence for the proposition in question; thus it always possible for any proposition to be false despite enormously strong inductive proof.

Deduction: For a valid argument, if the premises are true, the conclusion must be true.

Induction: For a strong argument, even if the evidence for the premises is all true, we may still doubt the conclusion.

Consider our quintessentially valid argument: ....
....

Valid Deduction:*

All men are mortal.
<u>Socrates is a man.</u>
Therefore, Socrates is mortal.

But is the above argument sound? How can we decide whether to believe the premises?

Very Strong Induction:

All the past humans we have
<u>ever heard of have been mortal.</u>
Therefore, all men are mortal.

Consider that it is impossible to have the kind of absolute certainty for this induction as we do for the above deduction. Why not? How can we doubt this? (How much do we know about *all* of the humans that have ever lived, are living, or will ever live? How can any claim about *all humans* be absolutely certain?)

It is clear that seeking absolute certainty when assessing the truth of any premise in an argument is an impossible expectation. Thus the truth of the premises for any argument must be evaluated within the dynamic context of the best evidence available, and how that is determined. Therefore, for the assessment of justification, very strong evidence for the premises and a valid deduction make for a sound argument.

Every argument has its deductive qualities in that deduction analyzes the form of the argument, i.e., how it is stated. Deduction is that part of every argument that takes us from the premises to the conclusion, and the success of the deduction is evaluated according to our definition of validity. Thus judging deduction is a fairly simple matter of determining the validity of the argument. Furthermore, because the definition of soundness is the basic criteria for judging arguments, if the argument is invalid, we needn't consider it further since it does not even have the deductive qualities necessary to lead to the conclusion. That is, an invalid argument does not fulfill one of the basic requirements for a sound argument; therefore the argument cannot be convincing, regardless of its other features.

The inductive side of every argument concerns the matter of truth: induction analyzes the truth of the argument's premises. It asks the question, "On what basis should we believe the reasons given in this argument?" Recall that "soundness" is the standard by which we judge an argument and an argument is sound if it is valid (referring to the deductive part of the argument) and its premises are true. Determining the truth of the premises is an important part of judging every argument, but while deduction is an entirely 'black and white' judgment, i.e., either the argument is valid or it is not (it's like being pregnant, an argument cannot be just a little bit valid), induction is far less certain. We must often consider the context of the evidence and the kind of claim it is supporting. The truth of the premises is determined by the relative *strength* of the evidence for each claim. That is, for each premise in an argument there is some evidence or justification for believing or disbelieving. The inductive assessment is an analysis of that evidence according to our understanding of the general standards for assessing evidence. This may not be as straight forward as our definition of validity, but we do have certain standards by which we can evaluate the evidence before us, e.g., the RET test.

The RET Test

Induction is a matter of the *strength* of the evidence. For most, the greatest difficulty in assessing an argument is determining whether the premises are true. This is why I suggest that validity be checked first, since it is often easier to determine. (Also, psychologically speaking, people are more likely to accept a mistake in their reasoning than a claim that one of their premises is false, i.e., that they might be lying.) Assessing evidence for a claim or premise is never easy due to the limits of our knowledge and our own interpretations of the world. It is never a clear cut issue. However there are recognized standards we can apply even to matters of truth and evidence, e.g., the RET test. RET stands for *relevance*, *enough* and *truth* of the evidence. That is, when evaluating the evidence for any claim in an argument, we should consider:

1. the *relevance* of the evidence to the claim being made;
2. the *quantity* of the evidence;

3. the relative *quality* of the evidence—the question of bias or prejudice toward one view or another.

Keep in mind, though the assessment of truth is not always clear, most people overwhelmingly agree about most matters (especially within the same culture). It is those few areas of disagreement that philosophy does most of its work--and where the fun is.

Evaluation of evidence should begin with some application of the **RET** test.

Let's begin with the following example: Someone tries two Canadian quarters in an U.S. pay telephone and it does not work (assuming local calls cost 50 cents). Should we conclude from this evidence that Canadian quarters do not work in U.S. pay telephones? If not, what evidence should convince us of the claim? Apply the RET test.

1. **R**elevance of the evidence. Is the evidence cited relevant to the claims being made? That is, we are sometimes given evidence for a claim that is not really related to that claim or is not related as to warrant that claim. Many informal fallacies are such because they violate this condition. In the above example, we can ask, is trying those two Canadian quarters in an U.S. pay telephone related as a source of evidence to the question of whether Canadian quarters generally work in U.S. pay telephones? The answer seems "yes" in this case.

2. **E**nough evidence. How much evidence or how many instances are required before we should accept a claim? Keep in mind, there are different standards for the amount of evidence for different kinds of claims. In the above example, we can ask, is this one attempt enough to warrant the conclusion that U.S. pay telephones do not accept Canadian quarters? This is where our example fails inductive standards of evidence. There seem to be two problems with the quantity of evidence. First, we should require more than one attempt on one pay telephone. Indeed, since we wish to draw a conclusion about U.S. pay telephones in general, it seems reasonable to demand that we try many pay telephones, geographically scattered across the United States. Second, we should require more than just those two Canadian quarters since it is possible that one or both is irregular in some way. Since we are also drawing a conclusion about Canadian quarters in general, we should try many Canadian quarters in each of the U.S. pay telephones.

Note how the above discussion only refers to increasing our quantity and distribution of evidence by 'many.' Although this suggests vagueness in our assessment of evidence, matters are not so unclear as one might expect. Although it would appear impossible to justify a precise quantification of such evidence, we can, by overall agreement due to the familiarity of the issue in question, determine an acceptable range of evidence within which to pursue our discussions. This may be the best we can hope for in most matters of truth, but it does establish an often surprising amount of agreement about evidentiary matters.

3. **T**ruth of the evidence. Can you trust the source of the evidence? Is there rational reason to doubt the veracity of the evidence or to suspect bias in its interpretation? Considering the information given in the above example, there seems little or no reason to doubt the veracity of the reports concerning the utility of Canadian quarters in U.S. telephones or to doubt the objectivity of the interpretation of the evidence. It is worth noting, however, that as an issue is more related to our values and sense of self, the questions of veracity and biased interpretation become more important.

Induction and deduction work together to make a sound argument. Making a good, sound argument is like making good orange juice. In the same way that good orange juice requires a good juicer, a sound argument requires a valid argument form. In the same way that good orange juice also requires good oranges, a sound argument also requires true (well-defended) premises.

Informal Fallacies

Philosophers have identified some general violations of the RET test that are frequently committed when assessing evidence for our claims. Informal Fallacies are distinguished from the Formal Fallacies discussed earlier by the fact that they are not so much problems with the form of the argument, but rather have to do with poor judgments of evidence and the like. I have listed below a few of the more common mistakes in reasoning; however this list is by no means exhaustive. Indeed, there are entire books and web sites dedicated to the various examples of improper evaluation about the truth of argument premises. Consider the following examples:

A. *Ad Hominem Fallacy/Genetic Fallacy* (both basically refer to the same error). It is a mistake to dismiss an argument merely because of who or where it comes from, but it is legitimate to consider the source when concerned with the question of bias in the evidence. Thus it seems prudent to be wary of legitimate ad hominem concerns of bias or false authority, even as we are being careful not to reject an argument outright just because of who is giving it. Example: It is wrong to dismiss arguments for the safety of tobacco merely because they come from the Tobacco Institute, but it is legitimate to consider this fact when determining if the evidence or data given is biased or misleading in some way.

B. *False Authority* or Appeal to Authority. We should always consider the following questions when a "truth" is supported only by an appeal to authority:

1. Is the cited authority actually an authority in the area under discussion ?

Example: Should we consider athletes to be experts on the subject of pain relievers?

2. Is this the kind of question that can be settled by an expert opinion ?

Example: Did you know that Albert Einstein, one of the foremost physicists of our time, predicted that atomic energy could not be harnessed for peaceful purposes?

3. Has the authority been cited correctly?

4. Can the authority be trusted to tell the truth?

Example: Would you trust a biologist who is also a devout Catholic to determine when life begins?

5. Why is an appeal to authority being made at all? Is this the only evidence for the claim? Is that enough?

C. *Circular Reasoning* or Begging the Question. Here the premises either merely repeat the conclusion or depend on its truth.

D. *Argument from Ignorance.* This is the attempt to prove a claim by observing that there is no evidence against it.

E. *False Dilemma.* This suggests that there are only two alternatives available (there are almost always more!).

F. *Slippery Slope* or "Camel's nose under the tent." Here it is suggested that because of a certain vagueness along a continuum, a distinction cannot be made between two points along the continuum. That is, once we start down a certain path we won't be able to stop because we cannot clearly justify any particular point along the continuum as the stopping place. This is a fallacy because it relies on vagueness of language rather than on facts to draw its conclusions, and vagueness of language is not relevant to such decisions. For example, since we cannot distinguish a baby at the moment of birth from a fetus one minute before birth, and it is always wrong to kill a baby, then it must also always be wrong to kill a fetus. That is, it is often argued that if we allow for abortion at any time during the pregnancy, there will be no rational justification to disallow abortions even very late in the pregnancy (e.g., in the last month). Therefore, we should not even get on this slippery slope, i.e., we should never allow for abortions. This kind of argument may seem convincing, but notice that we draw such distinctions all the time. For example, we say that someone must be 18 years old to vote because they are mature enough--but can you really distinguish the maturity of an 18 year old from a 17 year old? The point is we know that a distinction in maturity must be made and so we as a society just decide where to draw the line. This is the appropriate reply to any slippery slope argument.

G. *Straw Man Fallacy.* One misstates the opponent's position to make it easier to attack or sound ridiculous (politicians provide lots of examples of this fallacy!).

H. *Fallacies of Composition and Division.* These occur when we attempt to reason from characteristics of the parts to those of the whole (fallacy of composition) or from characteristics of the whole to those of the parts (fallacy of division). Example: My car is a Ford. Therefore, all of the components were made by Ford.

I. *Equivocation.* In equivocation a word or phrase changes meaning within the argument or discussion. Example: The apostles were twelve. That is very young to be an apostle.

J. *False Cause Fallacy.* Here one attributes a causal relation between things that are merely incidentally related. Example: Clinton became President after the fall of the Berlin Wall. Therefore, the fall of the Berlin Wall convinced us to vote for Clinton.

K. *Fallacy of Numbers.* This is to believe something because many others do as well.

L. *Argument ad Baculum.* Here one substitutes some form of physical coercion for reason in attempting to get others to agree to the claim.

M. *Appeal to Pity* and *Argumentum ad Populum*. Both of these fallacies attempt to replace the use of reason with the use of emotion to draw a conclusion.

N. *Hasty Generalization*. Too little evidence is provided to support the inductive conclusion.

O. *Complex Question*. This is another form of question-begging since it always assumes the proposition at issue in the premise of the question.

P. *Red Herring*. This fallacy occurs when someone purposely introduces irrelevancies to distract from the issue at hand (remember the RET test!).

Work the following Exercise 5 for Informal Fallacies on page 23 and then review your answers with Exercise 5 Answer Key—see page 34.

Only after you have attempted to work the exercises should you look at the Informal Fallacies Exercise Answer Key.

Exercise 6 will be assigned by your instructor.

Exercise 5: Informal Fallacies

Identify the Informal Fallacy committed in each argument.

1. Because the constituent cells of the human body are microscopic, the entire body is microscopic.

2. I would like to believe what you say about the inadvisability of the tuition raise, but I happen to know that you are a student, and it is clearly in your interest to oppose the increase.

3. The committee report is worthless. It has to be because the committee is composed of a bunch of idealistic intellectuals.

4. Business 301 must be a good course. Look at all the people taking it.

5. How can you say that Escorts are American cars when each part was made in a foreign country?

6. There must be ghosts because no one has been able to prove there aren't any.

7. If we allow the government to ban assault rifles, then next our hand guns will be taken from us. After that the government will ban our hunting rifles and shotguns. Pretty soon, we will not be allowed to carry pocket knives. Hence, all forms of gun control must be opposed.

8. Knowledge is power. Power corrupts. So knowledge corrupts.

9. "Each person's happiness is a good to that person, and the general happiness, therefore, a good to the aggregate of all persons." (J.S. Mill)

10. There is no evidence that Professor Hiccup is a poor teacher. Thus, he must be a decent teacher.

11. One should have sex only with those one loves. Parents love their children. Hence, parents should have sex with their children.

12. President Carter's policies were obviously inflationary. While he was in office, inflation grew to over 15% a year.

13. Either we build the MX missile systems or we give up all hope of arms control. We all desire arms control, so we must build the MX.

14. America: love it or leave it.

15. Don't believe Suzy about animal rights. She eats meat and wears leather.

Exercise 6: More Informal Fallacies

Identify the Informal Fallacy (if any) committed in each argument.

1. We should carefully consider Suzy's vegetarian arguments, but we should also remember that she works for the Soy Institute so there may be some bias in her data.

2. Either you're with us or against us!

3. We cannot question the Creationist account since there is no evidence to prove against it.

4. The members of that organization do great things, so the organization must be great.

5. We should embrace the most radical aspects of the Global Warming thesis since Al Gore promotes them.

6. Every time I wash my car it rains so I'm not going to wash my car this weekend.

7. "Yesterday I met a man with a wooden leg named Smith." "What was the name of his other leg?"

8. If voluntary euthanasia is allowed, eventually involuntary euthanasia will be permitted which will lead to a general disregard for life. So we should not allow any form of euthanasia.

9. Everybody thinks Wal-Mart has the best prices, so they must be the cheapest.

10. My dog always barks at the mailman, so all dogs bark at mail carriers.

11. You can't trust what he says about the environment, he drives an SUV.

12. This company is trustworthy and responsible to its customers, so John who works for the company must be trustworthy and responsible.

13. Every time we won a game I was wearing this shirt so this shirt must be lucky.

14. Either we increase mass transportation or continue to be dependent on foreign oil.

15. If we allow liquor sales on Sunday, it will just take sales from our Saturday business which is already taking away from Friday sales which takes from Thursday sales, etc. Therefore we should only be open on Monday.

On Scientific Hypotheses

Scientific hypotheses work in much the same way as Sound Arguments. Both rely on good evidence and observation and reason to be successful. Scientific explanations take the following form: (general principles) + (facts and initial conditions) = explanation of events in question. Notice the similarities between this form and that of the sound argument. That is, general principles often take a conditional form, e.g., if you bring water to 212 degrees Fahrenheit at sea level, then the water will boil. Statements of facts and initial conditions often take the form of subject/predicate statements like "the water is 212 degrees Fahrenheit at sea level" to explain the observation that the water is now boiling.

Although space does not permit an interesting, robust account of the analysis of scientific reasoning, it can be related to the application of the standards of reason. The following is another example of the application of scientific reasoning as analyzed by the form of reasoning discussed above (this is from a physical anthropology instructor I had as an undergraduate).

In the early 1950s, French Indochina experienced a sudden, unexplained epidemic of malaria in the highlands region. Malaria had never been a serious problem before in this area and anthropologists wanted an explanation for its sudden and dramatic appearance. The first general principle we might note is the social principle that "if confronted by a hostile, overwhelming force, a population will capitulate, die, or move."

Consider some facts and initial conditions. After WW2, many of the great colonial powers, including France, reasserted control over their colonies. Since the greatest value in the Indochina colony was the rubber plantations along the coastal areas, the French came in with overwhelming force to secure these areas for Michelin and other companies. Thus, we can hypothesize that many of the lowland Vietnamese moved to the highland region—and observation proved that correct.

A second general principle is when people migrate to a new area, they keep many of their previous ways of living (e.g., if you visit the Dutch East Indies, you'll find that the electrical outlets are always placed relatively high on the wall even though there is little chance of flooding in this region; however, there is a lot of flooding in the Netherlands from which the original colonists immigrated.). Here are some more facts and initial conditions. Coastal Vietnamese built their homes on the ground, cooked outside, and corralled their livestock away from the house; highland Vietnamese built their homes on stilts about 14' tall, cooked inside, and corralled their livestock beneath their homes. Thus we may conclude that the coastal Vietnamese continued to build their homes and live pretty much the way they had on the coast—and observation has shown this correct.

Some further facts and conditions are that malaria is vectored by the mosquito, mosquitoes do not like brackish water such as is found in a coastal area, mosquitoes cannot fly above about 14 feet, mosquitoes do not like smoky environments nor livestock. So the highlanders' way of living seems to discourage mosquito bites.

However, the coastal Vietnamese way of living, while adequate in the coastal areas not plagued with mosquitoes anyway, seems to encourage mosquito bites and the associated transmission of malaria. Thus we have an explanation of the sudden epidemic. This was further reinforced when the epidemic subsided after the French pulled out of Vietnam and displaced people began returning to their homes.

Do you see the application of the analysis of scientific reasoning in this account? Can you think of other scientific investigations that follow this or a similar pattern? Does the evidence pass the RET test?

On Analogy

Many arguments proceed by the use of analogy. An analogy works by citing a familiar and obvious line of reasoning that has characteristics similar to the topic at issue. The argument goes that since the two issues are similar and we know how to draw the proper inference in the obvious case, we should apply the same reasoning in the not-so-obvious case. That is, it draws its conclusion by suggesting that like things ought to be treated in a like manner. The general form of an analogy: A and B are similar via feature C. We conclude D about A. Therefore, we should also conclude D about B.

For example, consider the previous analogy about the relation between validity and truth in arguments. "Good orange juice (A) and sound arguments (B) are similar in that they both require good raw materials and processes (C) to start with. If bad oranges are used in the process, you get bad orange juice. Therefore, in like manner, if bad (untrue) premises are used in the argument, you get a bad (unsound) argument (D).

Of course, the similarity, I, between (A) and (B) must be relevant to (D) in order for the analogy to work as a valid form of reasoning. This intuition provides the basis for the standard by which we can judge any analogy. A good (sound) analogy must be based on 1) some actual similarity (C) between the two situations, and 2) that similarity (C) must be relevant to the conclusion (D) being drawn.

For example: Chess and football are both games. Football requires protective clothing. Therefore, by analogy, chess should require protective clothing. Where does this analogy go wrong? Consider the above standards for the judgment. Yes, chess and football are similar in that they are both games; however, the fact that they are both games does not seem to have anything to do with whether protective clothing is required. Thus the analogy fails on the question of relevance to the conclusion.

As you read through the various analogies given in the text, consider the above standards for evaluating them. Does the analogy pass these standards? Are the objections suggested by critics of the argument in some way related to the questions of relevance or similarity?
If so, exactly what is the question or problem for the analogy in question?

On Guarding Terms

In determining the truth of a particular premise, it is often necessary to consider how that claim is being guarded, if at all. That is, some words in our language serve to "guard" the proposition from easy falsification, thus making it more difficult to disagree with the claim. Examples of such words are "most," "some," "probably," "possibly," and "perhaps." As noted, the effect of such words in our sentences is to make those claims more difficult to disprove—thus they tend to be more believable.

There are two aspects to the use of guarding terms that are important in determining the soundness of arguments:

1. The more a proposition is guarded, the less likely that it can be shown to be false.
2. The more a proposition is guarded, the weaker the argument itself is, since the conclusion of any argument can never be any stronger than its weakest premise.

Consider the following example:

If I want to convince you that a particular snake lays eggs, I may argue that "All snakes lay eggs." Because of the universal quantifier "All" this is a very strong claim and would justify the conclusion that a particular snake lays eggs—i.e., it has a high level of certainty. But note that to disprove the premise "All snakes lay eggs" you need only find one snake that does not. Thus while the premise allows me to draw a very strong conclusion, it is relatively easy to disprove.

However, if I argue for the same conclusion that a particular snake lays eggs and only claim that "Most snakes lay eggs" in my argument, then the best conclusion I can reasonably draw is that that snake "probably" lays eggs—a much weaker (less certain) conclusion. But note that to disprove the premise "Most snakes lay eggs" you need to show that more than 50% of known species of snakes do not lay eggs—a far greater task than in the previous argument where only one exception was needed! Thus while the premise only allows me to draw a weak conclusion about what is probably the case (in relation to the snake), it is much more difficult to disprove.

Finally, if I argue that "Some snakes lay eggs," then the best conclusion I can draw is that the snake in question might lay eggs—note how weak (almost no certainty) this conclusion is! But also note that the premise "Some snakes lay eggs" is almost impossible to disprove since it would require showing that no snakes lay eggs. Thus while the premise allows very little certainty in our conclusion, it is almost completely guarded from any kind of falsification.

Therefore, when we are evaluating the soundness of an argument, we should take careful note of any guarding terms being used in the premises. We should determine how much the premise is guarded, i.e., how weak that premise is, and whether a stronger the conclusion has been drawn than is warranted by the premises. If the conclusion is much stronger than its weakest premise, then that is reason to reject the argument on grounds of validity since no weak premise can possibly lead to a strong conclusion. For example, "Some snakes lay eggs" can never, by itself, adequately justify the conclusion that "That snake must lay eggs." This also suggests just how intimate the relation between the issues of validity and truth really is—which is what has been said all along concerning the soundness of arguments!

On Suppressed Premises

An argument with unstated premises or conclusion is referred to as an *enthymeme*. Such arguments are more often the rule rather than the exception. In most cases, an enthymeme is a rather benign, as well as efficient, way to argue. That is, most justifications that leave out some premises or don't explicitly state their conclusion do so because those premises or conclusion are so obvious that it seems pedantic to state them. For example, if I argue "One needs a coat during the winter because it gets cold here," it seems too obvious to state that the function of a coat is to protect from the cold, even though this is the claim that connects the stated premise to the conclusion. We can legitimately assume that any reader or listener is already aware of such matters if she understands the language.

However, enthymemes are also given that are not so benign. These are arguments in which important premises are intentionally suppressed in order to avoid the kind of analysis that would show the argument to be unsound due to false or poorly supported premises. That is, some advocates recognize the weaknesses of their arguments and attempt to hide those weaknesses by leaving those premises unstated. Indeed, quite often such premises are precisely the claims that are most at issue and most in danger of being disproved.

Good critical thinkers look for such premises in order to fairly and properly evaluate the argument. For example, if I argue "Abortion is wrong because it kills an unborn child," I leave out some very important premises in the argument, i.e., "Conceptus and fetus are always unborn children" and "It is always wrong to kill." Although both such claims have some evidence and justification in their support, there is also good reason to examine them. Indeed, the argument seems to rest on these two premises in a very fundamental way such that these claims must be explicitly analyzed and evaluated.

Thus part of improving critical thinking is the practice of exposing suppressed premises. Most of the time, exposing a suppressed premise is merely to state the obvious. In this case, such is merely noted and the analysis continues with the rest of the argument. However, occasionally an important suppressed premise or assumption is exposed that either makes or breaks the argument. Indeed, this is a particularly important skill in philosophy and ethics where the arguments and topics are relatively complex and extended.

Exposing the suppressed premises of an argument proceeds via the basic standards of reason required by any justification, i.e., the validity of the argument and the truth of the premises. That is, a good critical thinker should ask: 1) is the argument valid? 2) if not, what statements should be added to make it valid? 3) are the premises true? 4) if not, what is needed to correct the premises? Answering these questions allows for the kind of complete analysis of the argument required for proper evaluation.

Consider the following example:

Argument 1.
P: Arnold Schwarzenegger was born in Austria.
_____
C: Therefore, Arnold Schwarzenegger cannot become President of the USA.

Note that this argument is invalid. Nothing explicitly stated in the premises rules out the possibility of a Schwarzenegger presidency. What premises must be added to make this argument valid?

Argument 2.
P1: Arnold Schwarzenegger was born in Austria.
P2: Austria has never been part of the United States.
P3: Someone who was born outside of the United States cannot be a native born U.S. citizen.
_____
C4: Therefore, Schwarzenegger is not a native born U.S. citizen.
P5: Only a native born U.S. citizen may become President of the United States.
C: Therefore, Arnold Schwarzenegger cannot become President of the USA.

Note that this argument is valid. However, P3 and P5 do not appear true since military dependents and others are sometimes born outside the United States and yet are still considered native born U.S. citizens and our first four presidents could not be U.S. citizens since the United States did not yet exist. How can we correct these premises?

Argument 3.
P1: Arnold Schwarzenegger was born in Austria.
P2: Austria has never been part of the United States.
P3: Schwarzenegger's parents were not United States citizens when he was born.
P4: Someone who was born outside of the United States and whose parents were not U.S. citizens when he/she was born cannot be a native born U.S. citizen.
C5: Therefore, Arnold Schwarzenegger is not a native born U.S. citizen.
P6: Arnold Schwarzenegger was born after ratification of the U.S. Constitution.
P7: Only a native born U.S. citizen or a U.S. citizen born before the adoption of the Constitution may become President of the United States.
C8: Therefore, Arnold Schwarzenegger cannot become President of the USA.

Note that a two statement argument has become eight statements merely by exposing those premises necessary to meet our basic standards of reason. Thus by exposing all of the suppressed premises, we can properly analyze and evaluate the argument.

Work the following Exercise 7: Suppressed Premises on page 31.

Only after you have attempted to work the exercises should you look at the Suppressed Premises Exercise Answer Key—see p. 35.

Exercise 7: Suppressed Premises

<u>Expose the suppressed premise(s) in each of the following arguments.</u>

1. Nixon couldn't have been president in 1950 since he was still in the Senate.

2. 81 is not a prime number because 81 is divisible by 3.

3. There's no one named Rupert here; we have only female patients.

4. Columbus did not discover the New World because the Vikings explored Newfoundland centuries earlier.

5. If there were survivors, they would have been found by now.

6. Lincoln could not have met Washington because Washington was dead before Lincoln was born.

7. Philadelphia cannot play Los Angeles in the World Series since they are both in the National League.

8. Mildred must be over 43 since she has a daughter who is 36.

9. He cannot be grandfather because he never had children.

10. That's not acid rock; you can understand the lyrics.

11. Harold can't play in the Super Bowl because he broke his leg

12. Britney Spears is under 35. Therefore, she cannot run for president of the United States.

13. Minute must be a basketball player since he's so tall.

14. Susan refuses to work on Sundays, which shows she is lazy and inflexible.

15. Dan is either stupid or very cunning, so he must be stupid.

16. Jim told me that Bathsheba is a professor, so she can't be a student since professors must already have degrees.

17. SDI will never work unless we are very lucky or the Russians are friendly, so we can't rely on it.

18. SDI will never work because it will require powerful lasers which we cannot even begin to build at this time.

Exercises 1 Answer Key

Determine: 1) Which of the following is an argument and 2) Which of the arguments is valid according to the definition of validity.

a) Most cats are smart. Garfield is a cat. So, Garfield must be smart.

This is an argument—notice the conclusion marker 'So'. However, it is not valid. Since it says that only 'most' cats are smart, it is possible that Garfield is not smart.

b) Either I will go to the party tonight or I will study at the library. Since I'm not going to the party, I will be studying at the library.

This also is an argument—notice the reason marker 'Since.' This is also a valid argument since there is no way to believe the premises and not believe that I will be studying at the library. What valid argument form is being used?

c) You can fool some of the people all of the time, and all of the people some of the time. But you can't fool all of the people all of the time.

This is not an argument. There are no warranting connectives and none of these claims may be seen as reason for holding the other.

d) All dogs are dumb. Snoopy is a dog. So, Snoopy must be dumb.

This is an argument—notice the conclusion marker 'So.' The argument is valid. What valid argument form is being used?

e) If the election were held today, Kerry would win. But the election is not being held today. So, Kerry will not win.

This is an argument—notice the if-then pattern and the conclusion marker 'So.' But consider that nothing in the premises rules out the possibility of Kerry winning on some other day, hence this is an invalid argument. What formal fallacy is committed here?

f) If the election were held today, Bush would win. But Bush is not winning. So, the election must not be held today.

This is an argument—notice the if-then pattern and the conclusion marker 'So.' This is a valid argument. What valid argument form is being used?

Exercise 3: Argument Forms Exercises Answer Key

1. Modus Tollens

2. Disjunctive Syllogism

3. Modus Ponens

4. Disjunctive Syllogism

5. Formal Fallacy—Denying the Antecedent

6. Disjunctive Syllogism

7. Formal Fallacy—Denying the Antecedent

8. Modus Tollens

9. Disjunctive Syllogism **and** Modus Tollens

10. Disjunctive Syllogism **and** Formal Fallacy—Denying the Antecedent

11. Hypothetical Syllogism

12. Formal Fallacy—Affirming the Consequent

13. Universal Syllogism

Exercise 5: Informal Fallacies Exercises Answer Key

1. Fallacy of Composition

2. Ad Hominem Fallacy

3. Ad Hominem Fallacy

4. Fallacy of Numbers

5. Fallacy of Composition

6. Argument from Ignorance

7. Slippery Slope

8. Equivocation

9. Fallacy of Composition

10. Argument from Ignorance

11. Equivocation

12. False Cause Fallacy

13. False Dilemma Fallacy

14. False Dilemma Fallacy

15. Ad Hominem Fallacy

Exercise 7: Suppressed Premises Exercise Answer Key

1. One cannot simultaneously be president of the United States and a United States Senator.

2. Prime numbers are only divisible by 1 and themselves.

3. Rupert is only a male name.

4. A discoverer must be the first and Newfoundland is part of the New World.

5. No survivors have been found.

6. One cannot meet someone after she dies.

7. The World Series is a competition between National League and American League champions.

8. A woman must be older than 7 years to bear a child.

9. Only a parent can be a grandparent.

10. Acid rock lyrics cannot be understood.

11. One cannot play football with a broken leg and the Super Bowl is a football game.

12. One must be over 35 years old to run for president of the United States.

13. All tall people play basketball.

14. If one refuses to work on Sunday, she is either lazy or inflexible.

15. Dan is not very cunning.

16. Those with degrees cannot be students.

17. There are only two alternatives and we will not be lucky, nor will the Russians be friendly.

18. If we cannot build something now, we never will.